HANNAH BAILEY   KITSON JAZYNKA

EXPLORE!
AMERICA'S
WILDLIFE

For all young readers who love wild animals as much as I do—KJ

Thank you to my husband Aidan, for your unwavering support, and to my Grandpa, Jack—HB

YOSEMITE

TOP 10 camp grounds

MAP

First American Edition 2023
Kane Miller, A Division of EDC Publishing

Text copyright © Macmillan Publishers International Limited 2023
Illustrations copyright © Hannah Bailey 2023
Published under license from Kingfisher, Pan Macmillan, a division of
Macmillan Publishers International Limited, London, United Kingdom.
The right of Hannah Bailey to be identified as the illustrator
of this work has been asserted.

Senior design: Jeni Child
Design assistant: Amelia Brooks
Senior editor: Lizzie Davey
Additional illustrations: Nic Jones and Suzanne Washington

For information contact:
Kane Miller, A Division of EDC Publishing
5402 S 122nd E Ave, Tulsa, OK 74146
www.kanemiller.com
Library of Congress Control Number: 2022938834
Printed and bound in China
1 2 3 4 5 6 7 8 9 10
ISBN: 978-1-68464-471-1

Kane Miller
A DIVISION OF EDC PUBLISHING

MIX
Paper | Supporting
responsible forestry
FSC® C116313

Picture credits
The Publisher would like to thank the following for permission to reproduce
their material.
25 H. Mark Weidman Photography/Alamy Stock Photo; 31 Bob Gibbons/Alamy Stock Photo;
44 Stephen Bonk/Shutterstock; 45 Chris Mattison/Alamy Stock Photo; 47 Nathan A
Shepard/Shutterstock; 52 US Army Photo/Alamy Stock Photo; 55 Nature Picture Library/
Alamy Stock Photo; 58 Kip Evans/Alamy Stock Photo; 59 Stephen Bonk/Alamy Stock
Photo; 72 Howard Sandler/Shutterstock; 73 Chris Hill/Shutterstock; 86 Rolf Hicker
Photography/Alamy Stock Photo; 87 Custom Life Science Images/Alamy Stock Photo;
89 Raymond Hennessy/Alamy Stock Photo.

HANNAH BAILEY   KITSON JAZYNKA

EXPLORE!
AMERICA'S
WILDLIFE

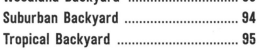

THE UNITED STATES

The United States is a place of great diversity. It's a land made up of different environments and habitats, from sandy deserts to muggy or foggy coastal cities, snowcapped mountains, grassy valleys, lakes, and forest. There are nearly 3,000 species of native animals—including mammals, birds, reptiles, amphibians, and fish—and about 18,000 types of naturally occurring plants. In this book, you'll get to know some of those plants and animals. We've divided the book into four geographical regions: West, Midwest, South, and Northeast.

MIDWEST

New Hampshire
Maine
Vermont
Massachusetts
Rhode Island
Connecticut
New Jersey

Washington
North Dakota
Minnesota
Montana
Wisconsin
Oregon
South Dakota
Michigan
New York
Idaho
Wyoming
Iowa
Pennsylvania
NORTHEAST
Nevada
Nebraska
Illinois
Indiana
Ohio
West Virginia
Delaware
Maryland
Utah
Colorado
Virginia
District of Columbia
California
Kansas
Missouri
Kentucky
North Carolina
Arizona
New Mexico
Tennessee
South Carolina
Oklahoma
Arkansas
Georgia
Mississippi
Alabama
Louisiana
Texas
Florida

WEST

SOUTH

Hawaii
US Virgin Islands

Alaska

American Samoa

WONDERFUL AND WILD

The phrase "native species" refers to plants and animals that occur naturally (or without human intervention) in a particular place. These species contribute to a healthy habitat.

Native oak trees in certain areas of the United States can support hundreds of species of caterpillars. Non-native trees planted in the same areas support only a few types of caterpillars.

Native species, such as the beaver, are found in multiple areas (in this case the United States, Europe, and Asia), and are considered "indigenous."

Other specialized native species rely on particular conditions and survive in only one location on Earth. Pygmy rabbits inhabit Oregon, California, Nevada, Utah, Idaho, Montana, Washington, and Wyoming. The model cave harvestman (a spider relative) can be found only in the Great Basin region of Nevada.

Native chickadees need thousands of caterpillars to feed their young. Invasive species can change the habitat or deplete food sources.

TIPS FOR WILDLIFE WATCHING

Spot this!

With permission, check out online wildlife cams to watch animals such as wolves, grizzly bears, and nesting bald eagles.

Stay safe!

Never follow an animal to snap a picture. Instead, use binoculars or a camera lens to see them up close.

Track this!

Look for signs of wild animals wherever you go. If you find an animal track in the mud, look at the shape, and think about the animal that might have left it. What direction was it going, and why?

Spot this!

Be outside at dawn, dusk, and around the times of incoming tides to increase your chances of seeing mammals, birds, and fish.

HABITATS

The word "habitat" refers to the different natural environments where plants and animals live. The United States has a wide range of these places, from dry, hot deserts to wet marshlands and freezing cold polar habitats.

COASTAL HABITAT

Areas along or near a shoreline

FORESTS

Land mostly covered with trees and brush

SUBURBAN ENVIRONMENT

The region surrounding a city

CORAL REEF

Underwater ocean environment

DESERTS
Arid lands with little rainfall

WETLANDS
Swampy or marshy areas where much of the land is saturated or underwater

PRAIRIE
Rolling, fertile grasslands

WORDS TO KNOW

Flora
The plants of a particular region

Fauna
The animals of a particular region

Vertebrates
Animals with backbones, made up of five main groups: fish, amphibians, reptiles, birds, and mammals

Invertebrates
Animals without backbones such as earthworms, jellyfish, squid, butterflies, and other insects

Native species
Plants and animals that occur naturally in a place, without human intervention

Indigenous species
Native species that are adaptable and can be found in different areas

Endemic species
Native species that survive only under special conditions or in a particular habitat, which could be an entire island, a particular body of water, or a certain elevation on a mountain range where a specific plant grows

KATMAI

BERING SEA

NORTH
CASCADES

REDWOOD
FORESTS

GREAT PLAINS

SHEEP LAKES

MONTEREY BAY

GREAT PLAINS

CALIFORNIA
CHAPARRAL

CABEZA
PRIETA

THE WEST
AND ALASKA

The western United States covers a huge range of territory with diverse ecosystems, from dry deserts to damp rain forests and everything in between. When Sacajawea, a member of the Shoshone tribe, guided explorers Meriwether Lewis and William Clark across the uncharted lands of the American West in the 1800s, they encountered harsh weather and unforgiving terrain. They also observed and documented many species of unfamiliar plants, including blue flax, and animals such as bighorn sheep, bison, grizzly bears, the northern pocket gopher, and the brown-headed cowbird. Flip the page and lace up your hiking boots to start your own journey. You'll learn about the amazing animals and plants that inhabit this big, beautiful part of the world. Which favorites will you write home about?

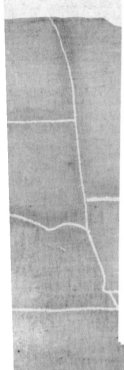

BERING SEA

1

2

3

4

5

4

DID YOU KNOW?

Many endangered whales live wild, watery lives in the Bering Sea. This includes the blue whale, the sperm whale, and the North Pacific right whale.

6

Key

1. Polar bear
2. Walrus
3. Spectacled eider
4. Least auklet
5. Beluga whale
6. North Pacific right whale

Polar bears in the Bering Sea survive by eating "ice seals." There are four seal species in this group: bearded seals, ringed seals, spotted seals, and ribbon seals. A polar bear might rest beside a seal's breathing hole in the ice, then wait for it to surface.

Spotted seal

Ribbon seal

Spot these!

Bearded seal

The Bering Sea is one of the coldest bodies of water on the planet. The plants and animals that live here must tolerate strong winds, icy water, and temperatures as low as -49°F. Fish such as herring, cod, flounder, and salmon thrive in the area, which draws fishing boats. Sea otters and fur seals use islands here for their breeding grounds. Whales, walruses, and sea lions live among the floating ice, along with hundreds of species of fish and seabirds.

Snap this!

Imagine that!

Bamboo corals thrive in cold, dark water, and can be found in two-mile-deep underwater canyons at the bottom of the Bering Sea. These bioluminescent animals form "trees" at the ocean bottom, growing up to three feet high. They provide shelter for reef fish and invertebrates.

Like most Bering Sea inhabitants, walruses excel at swimming. Hind flippers propel them as they dive to the seafloor to snag mollusks and invertebrates. They rest on slippery ice floes between hunting trips.

Ringed seals are the smallest seal in the Arctic. They live their lives in water and on ice. Snow-covered lairs, or "snow caves," protect mothers and babies from the cold, and also from hungry polar bears.

Spot this!

13

2

3

4

DID YOU KNOW?

Katmai National Park sits at the northeastern end of the Alaska Peninsula. This fingerlike piece of land points into the North Pacific Ocean, and is home to more brown bears than people.

5

6

KATMAI

Katmai National Park is a vast, remote, and wild place, spanning more than four million acres of astonishing land. It is the perfect home for thousands of brown bears, which feed on the salmon that splash and spawn in Katmai's untamed rivers and streams. The volcanoes in Katmai are part of the "Ring of Fire"—a chain of volcanic mountains that surrounds the Pacific Ocean. The area includes the Valley of Ten Thousand Smokes, a place that was created by lava flows and ash. Katmai also has tundra areas where it is too cold for trees and forests to grow.

Key

1. Marten
2. Sitka spruce
3. Caribou
4. Arctic wolf
5. Brown bear
6. Beaver
7. River otter
8. Snowshoe hare
9. Weasel

BROWN BEAR

Brown bears are huge, burly carnivores that dominate this cold landscape. When sockeye salmon travel upstream, the bears gather at waterfalls. They wait for the fish to leap, then try to grab them.

Long claws allow brown bears to dig for roots and catch salmon.

Brown bear colors range from dark brown to light blond.

Brown bears are excellent swimmers and can dive underwater to catch fish.

A brown bear in Katmai might eat dozens of sockeye salmon in a single day. They eat the fattiest parts of the fish first.

Spot this!

Katmai is the perfect home for Canada lynx, which tend to avoid humans. These silvery cats have large, wide feet that enable them to walk on the surface of the snow. They prey almost exclusively on snowshoe hares, which spend their whole lives trying to avoid these relentless predators.

Wow!

Wolverines, also known as skunk bears, are curious and tough. They'll do anything to find food, from climbing trees or an ice wall to heading straight down a mountain in a storm.

Snap this!

Colorful flowers bloom on Katmai's tundra, including narcissus-flowered anemone, Arctic willow, woolly lousewort, and alpine azalea.

Alutiiq people, native to Alaska, call black-capped chickadees "Uksullaq," which means "winter one." These little birds work hard to consume enough fat to survive Katmai's cold nights. They also fluff their feathers, to create a layer of warm air.

Check this out!

1

1

2

3

4

NORTH CASCADES

Key

1 Bald eagle
2 Moose
3 Gray wolf
4 Checkerspot butterfly
5 Canada lynx
6 Mountain goat

Washington's wild and majestic North Cascades mountains are sometimes called the "American Alps." The area is famous for its snowcapped peaks, raging rivers, alpine meadows, and densely forested valleys. Wolves, lynx, and moose call this place home.

MOUNTAIN LION

Mountain lion kittens rely on their mother for food, protection, and warmth. She communicates with soft purrs and stays with them day and night until they are about 10 days old. Soon after, she resumes solo hunting, perhaps for mule deer or porcupine. When the kittens are older they follow, watch, and learn.

A mountain lion kitten's spots help it hide from danger.

A mountain lion's den might be hidden by a fallen Douglas fir tree, and surrounded by a nearly impenetrable patch of prickly currant. This protects the cubs from predators such as bears and wolves when the mother leaves the den to hunt.

Wow!

Bats are the only mammal that can truly fly. At least eight species of bats are found in the North Cascades, including the western small-footed bat, which weighs as little as four grams.

Hear this!

Hoary marmots are social animals common in the higher forest elevations. They whistle to warn others if predators, such as golden eagles or coyotes, are nearby.

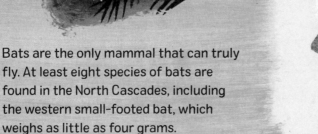

Spot this!

Ungulates, or hoofed animals, in this area include elk, mule deer, moose, and solitary mountain goats that climb on rocks.

Discover this!

North American beavers are large rodents that can swim fast underwater, powered by their webbed back feet. Broad, paddle-like tails help them steer. They can stay underwater for up to 15 minutes, and have eyelids that work like goggles.

REDWOOD FORESTS

What's it like to stand under a 1,000-year-old tree that's almost as tall as the Statue of Liberty? Redwood forests are some of the few places in the world where you can find out. Look up in these misty temperate rain forests, and you'll see reddish-brown bark stretching up under drooping branches heavy with long, thin leaves as far as you can see.

Key

1. Raccoon
2. Pacific giant salamander
3. Banana slug
4. California slender salamander
5. Coyote
6. Northern spotted owl

DID YOU KNOW?
Redwood trees are massive, but their pine cones are tiny—about an inch long, or the size of a bottle cap.

Mini communities of plants made up of as many as a hundred species can live on a single redwood tree. They include mosses, lichens, and other plants.

Marbled murrelets—
endangered seabirds—
seek out the tallest,
oldest redwood trees.
There, they nest
on large, flat
branches with soft,
cushioning moss
for the single
eggs they lay.

Needlelike leaves look similar to pine needles, but are softer than those found on most other evergreen trees.

REDWOOD TREE

Redwood trees are among the biggest and oldest in the world. These majestic and important trees help fight climate change, and provide a home for many smaller plants and animals.

Pacific tailed frogs are endemic to the Pacific Northwest, meaning it's the only place these tiny, voiceless frogs are found on Earth. Their tadpoles have mouths that work like suction cups. This helps them cling to rocks, to avoid getting swept away in the gushing stream environments where they live.

Watch this!

Spy this!

Redwood stubble is a lichen species as tiny as its host tree is huge. A lichen is a slow-growing organism that lives on rocks, walls, and trees. Other types might look crusty, bumpy, or leafy, but this kind of lichen sprouts from redwood bark like little hairs.

Spot this!

Long and sleek, the Pacific fisher is a fierce and hard-to-find member of the weasel family. Despite their name, fishers don't eat fish but hunt small animals such as hares, rodents, and birds. They also attack porcupines, providing that they can do so face-to-face and avoid the sharp quills.

Find this!

Thousands of huge Roosevelt elk roam Pacific Northwest forests. A century ago, humans nearly hunted this beautiful species to extinction. The elk graze on the forests' ferns, shrubs, and lichens, as well as grasses in the surrounding meadows.

Key

1 Jeweled top snail
2 Garibaldi
3 California sea otter
4 Giant green anemone
5 Purple sea urchin
6 Bat star
7 California sea lion
8 Leopard shark

DID YOU KNOW?

Kelp fronds have hollow, globe-shaped growths on their leaflike blades that help them rise toward the sun. A rootlike structure called a "holdfast" anchors the kelp to the ocean floor.

MONTEREY BAY

A kelp forest is like an underwater jungle without any trees. These forests are often found in the cool waters along the western coast of the United States. They are lush, dense ecosystems, made up of giant brown algae that grow and sway with the currents in shallow, cool water close to shore. This protective sunlit area provides shelter and food for an unbelievable number of fish, invertebrates such as octopuses, and marine mammals such as sea otters. Some kelp species can grow to be as tall as a 15-story building.

RED OCTOPUS

Red octopuses are intelligent animals with eight sucker-covered tentacles used for grabbing, walking, tasting, touching, and manipulating shells as tools.

To attract a mate, a red octopus might turn a bright color, so it stands out. To hide, it can match itself to look like the color and texture of its surroundings, such as sand or rocks.

A red octopus eats mollusks, fish, and crustaceans such as small crabs.

After it eats, the red octopus deposits its empty shells outside its den in a pile, or an "octopus's garden."

The red octopus kills prey with venom. It then cracks the shells with its sharp beak or makes a hole in them with its drill-like tooth or "radula."

Snap this!

Sea otters rely on the kelp forest for protection and food. Adult otters wrap themselves in kelp fronds for safety, and mother otters wrap their babies up so they don't float away.

Discover this!

Gray whales sometimes seek refuge among the kelp, likely hiding from hungry orcas. While there, the whale might snack on invertebrates including brittle stars, bristle worms, and prawns, as well as crabs and other crustaceans.

Watch this!

The brown turban is a small snail that lives in the kelp forest. It eats by licking microscopic algae off the surface of the kelp. If it gets stuck upside down on the ocean floor it can use a pebble to roll itself over.

Find this!

Leopard sharks swish through the dappled sunlight of the kelp forest. They eat squid, prawns, crabs, and innkeeper worms. Schools of these sleek, beautiful sharks follow the tides as they feed.

29

CALIFORNIA CHAPARRAL

DID YOU KNOW?

You can explore chaparral landscape on the many rolling trails around much of Southern California.

California's chaparral is defined by areas of shrubby woodlands, often in the foothills of mountains. Stands of these "shrublands" are made up of native, drought-resistant plants that have hard leaves that hold moisture. The chaparral environment pops up in areas with hot, dry summers and mild, wet winters.

The state bird of California, the California quail is a common chaparral resident and makes a call that sounds like "chi-ca-go." These birds spend their time on the ground, scratching for food under or near shrubs. They travel in groups called "coveys" and fly in bursts just big enough to get from one bush to the next.

Key

1 California condor
2 California mantis
3 Black-tailed jackrabbit
4 Ladybug
5 Southern alligator lizard
6 Ceanothus silk moth
7 Coast horned lizard
8 Western scrub jay

Hear this!

Find this!

Timemas are short, stout stick insects, related to walking sticks. They are wingless and can't fly, but feed on plants like chamise, and look like branches, to disguise themselves from predators.

Spot this!

Discover this!

Chamise, or greasewood, is related to the rose plant and is the chaparral's most common shrub. Its flowering branches provide shelter and food for native butterflies, moths, and birds.

Huge, endangered California condors scrape up leaves and bark to create nests with thick bedding for their large eggs. Condor eggs can be double the size of chicken eggs.

Key

1 Gila woodpecker
2 Western diamondback rattlesnake
3 Roadrunner
4 Cactus wren
5 Mojave rattlesnake

CABEZA PRIETA

Cabeza Prieta National Wildlife Refuge is a stunning but isolated and sometimes hostile desert wilderness. The refuge is made up of rugged mountains, arid valleys, sand dunes, and two-million-year-old lava flows. Saguaro cactus sprout from this baked earth and offer both refuge and a little moisture to native wildlife.

SAGUARO CACTUS

These colossal cactus can reach 70 feet high and have been known to live for 150 years. They are a key source of food, shelter, and even water for the animals that live alongside them. At night, the lesser long-nosed bat feeds on the saguaro's nectar and fruit, then helps to spread the cacti's seeds.

Gila woodpeckers live in the Sonoran Desert year round. They carve holes in the pulpy flesh of these cacti. The holes are sometimes later inhabited by elf owls or sparrows.

Jackrabbits, mule deer, and other animals stay hydrated by feeding on young saguaro if they can't find water.

Track this!

The Sonoran pronghorn has adapted to its arid environment by being smaller and lighter in color than other pronghorn antelopes. Its hair also helps the species to cope with extreme temperatures—it stiffens up and lifts to release body heat.

Watch this!

Racing roadrunners are fun to watch in the Sonoran Desert. These speedsters can sprint at up to 15 miles per hour in pursuit of snakes, insects, lizards, rodents, and smaller birds. These entertaining birds are part of the cuckoo family.

Hot, dry conditions in the Sonoran Desert make it an ideal home for side-blotched and desert horned lizards. There are also six species of rattlesnakes here, including sidewinders, Mojave, and western diamondback rattlers.

Beware this!

Spot this!

The cactus wren is the state bird of Arizona. It nests in barbed cholla, using dried grasses and scraps of cloth to create a football-shaped home with an opening at one end. The plant's uninviting needlelike spines discourage whipsnakes (which have an appetite for eggs) as well as predators that prey on adult birds.

Key

1 Rocky Mountain bighorn sheep
2 North American elk
3 Red-tailed chipmunk
4 Mountain bluebird

DID YOU KNOW?

Bighorn sheep are more nervous around humans than other hooved wild species such as elk or deer. Park rangers often stop traffic to let the sheep pass without disturbance from cars or curious humans.

SHEEP LAKES

Spotting wildlife is one of the many great things to do on a visit to Sheep Lakes in Rocky Mountain National Park. During the summer you can catch a glimpse of Rocky Mountain bighorn sheep coming down from the mountains to visit Sheep Lakes. They flock to this area not to swim, but to lick the mineral-rich mud or "salt licks" at the edges of the area's small lakes.

BIGHORN SHEEP

The Rocky Mountain bighorn sheep is the state animal of Colorado. It is massive, fleecy, and has huge curling horns. These sure-footed animals live in herds and survive by eating grass, seeds, and plants.

Bighorn sheep live on steep mountain slopes—even on slopes that seem to go straight up.

Bighorn males, called rams, use their impressive heavy horns as weapons in epic, noisy battles during the mating season.

Lambs are born each spring on high, secluded ledges. The parents must protect their playful and independent offspring from predators, including wolves and golden eagles.

Spot this!

American pikas are furry mammals that also live on grass and plants, and share the bighorn sheep's high mountain habitat. Both species are endangered.

Key

1 Bison
2 Chestnut-collared longspur
3 Western meadowlark

GREAT PLAINS

Ancient glaciers flattened this great stretch of land. It spans ten states, stretching vertically from north to south across the center of the US. Grasslands carpet the region, providing a home for wildlife, including many important bird species that might soon be extinct such as mountain plovers, burrowing owls, and chestnut-collared longspurs.

DID YOU KNOW?

Bison are the heaviest land animals in North America. They are massive but still quick on their feet, and can run in bursts of up to 35 miles per hour.

Discover this!

Millions of bison once roamed this beautiful landscape. Today, most of Earth's bison live in managed herds. These powerful herbivores help plants by aerating soil with their huge hooves, and spreading plant seeds as they graze.

Spot this!

American badgers are ideally suited to dig in the dirt. Huge front claws make them expert excavators, digging out burrows that can be 10 feet deep and 6 feet wide. When hunting prairie dogs, badgers sometimes partner with coyotes. Coyotes can find prairie dogs, but can't dig them out. They wait outside while the badger digs.

During spring and summer, burrowing owls nest and roost in abandoned burrows left behind by badgers, prairie dogs, or other small mammals. These little owls often "redecorate," lining their homes with feathers and bits of grass. They also spread animal manure outside, to attract small animals and insects: easy prey.

Look at this!

Find this!

These grasslands are home to the rarest mammal in North America, the black-footed ferret. Black-footed ferrets were once thought to be extinct, and conservationists are working to improve their numbers. Black-footed ferrets live in prairie dog colonies. Each ferret eats around 100 prairie dogs a year.

The Southern United States is home to incredible animals. They include endangered red wolves in North Carolina, the remarkable Virginia opossum (North America's only marsupial), and the formidable black diamond rattlesnake. The region is known for heat, humidity, and lots of sunshine. It has lush, swampy landscapes such as the Savannah National Wildlife Refuge in South Carolina, where visitors can see alligators, turtles, and dragonflies live out their lives in fragrant aquatic "fields" of water lilies.

In southern cities people and wildlife live alongside each other. For example, Charlotte and Raleigh, cities in North Carolina, are both part of the Butterfly Highway, a state program that teaches homeowners how to grow native gardens to attract pollinators. In Dallas, humans share their backyards with local bobcats. Manatees in Tampa flock to warm water created by the local power plant, which has a viewing deck for people eager to admire these whiskery wild animals.

THE SOUTH

CHINCOTEAGUE

SALT PLAINS

CANAAN VALLEY

FERN CAVE

MISSISSIPPI SANDHILL CRANE REFUGE

CRYSTAL RIVER

FLORIDA PANTHER REFUGE

CHINCOTEAGUE

1

Sun, salty ocean air, and breezy marsh grass greet you when you arrive in this popular refuge in Virginia. Located on the southern end of Assateague Island, this pristine place is home to famous spotted ponies. It's also a refuge for many other animals that live in and around the island's sandy beaches, salt marshes, maritime forests, and bays. Look for wading birds, fiddler crabs, and mud turtles. Don't forget your camera and your bug spray!

2

DID YOU KNOW?

Each July, the Chincoteague ponies swim across a narrow channel from Assateague Island to Chincoteague, herded by a group of "saltwater cowboys." The cowboys lead the ponies in a mud-splattered parade down the town's Main Street before the annual Chincoteague Pony Auction.

3

4

5

Key

1. Laughing gull
2. Chincoteague pony
3. Diamondback terrapin
4. Blue crab
5. Eastern box turtle
6. Great egret
7. Virginia opossum
8. Delmarva Peninsula fox squirrel

43

Chincoteague ponies are small, sturdy, and shaggy. They have lived on Assateague Island for hundreds of years. Some say the herds arrived on Assateague when early settlers let their ponies graze free. Others say that today's ponies are descendants of ponies who survived when a ship sunk off the island's coast.

Meet this!

Spot these!

Horseshoe crabs have been around since long before the dinosaurs. These strange, spiny-legged creatures are more closely related to spiders than they are to other crabs. If you spot one upside down, gently pick it up by the shell and turn it over near the surf. Never grab one by the tail! These fascinating animals can live for 20 years or more.

The plump, fluffy Delmarva Peninsula fox squirrel is the largest tree squirrel in North America. It has a super-long, bushy tail, which works as a snug blanket to wrap up in when it's cold. This silvery species is more timid than the familiar gray squirrel, and quite a bit bigger.

Find this!

Watch this!

You'll find lots of cool crustaceans in this place, most common of which are crabs. Tiny hermit crabs burrow into the sand at your feet. Male fiddler crabs have one claw much larger than the other, to defend their burrows and impress females. Ghost crabs (shown here) are nocturnal—they only come out at night.

Spot this!

The diamondback terrapin is a small turtle found on the East Coast of the United States. A diamond-shaped pattern covers its scutes—the bony plates on its shell. This species was almost hunted to extinction by 19th-century humans, who liked to eat turtle soup.

Discover this!

The Virginia opossum is not known for its beauty, but it's very important to its environment. The possum's diet includes ticks, which spread disease to many animals, including humans. Another cool thing about these small mammals? They are the only marsupial (mammal with a pouch, like a kangaroo) in North America.

The sea star is often called a "starfish," but it's not a fish. It's an invertebrate, related to sea cucumbers and sea urchins. These animals are all echinoderms, which have spiny skins to protect them from predators. To get around, sea stars have rows of tiny tube feet that allow them to crawl along the ocean floor, using suction.

Hear these!

The laughing gull breeds in Virginia and is a common summer sight in this sunny refuge. It glides overhead on the beach, darting after scraps of food left by humans, and skimming above the water in flocks of a hundred or more. Listen for their rowdy, cackling calls.

Wow!

CANAAN VALLEY

The elevated peaks of the Allegheny Mountains cradle this cool, misty valley. Winters are snowy here, while summers stay cool. Bogs, swamps, and wet meadows carpet the valley floor. The rugged area's chilly climate is similar to Maine or Canada, and the plants and animals here do well in cold conditions. Animals include deer, raccoons, geese, barred owls, mink, frogs, and salamanders. The valley's flowering plants feed many of those animals, including hummingbirds and large numbers of butterflies in the summer.

Look for this!

Rough-legged hawks hunt in this area during the winter. These large birds swoop in to catch the many small mammals that live in the Canaan Valley grasslands. They return to the Arctic tundra for the summer.

Wow!

Groundhogs (also known as woodchucks) fill up on food during the spring, summer, and fall, then hibernate in the cold winter months. During their hibernation, they sleep and wake in a groggy cycle. In February, the groundhogs wake up and leave their burrows to search for mates.

Key

1 White-tailed deer
2 Common whitetail dragonfly
3 Raccoon
4 Common buckeye butterfly
5 Pipevine swallowtail butterfly
6 Spring peeper
7 Bar-winged skimmer

Spot this!

The small, slender Cheat Mountain salamander lives in red spruce and yellow birch trees in the Allegheny Mountains. This species is considered endemic to the area because it isn't found anywhere else on Earth. When hungry snakes, short-tailed shrews, or other predators try to hunt this salamander, it produces a smelly, slimy chemical on its skin to discourage them.

Snap this!

The cardinal flower is a bright-red wildflower that grows in the Canaan Valley's shady, wet marshes and on stream banks. Hummingbirds drink nectar from its tubular flowers throughout the summer.

CRYSTAL RIVER

In the winter, the blue waters of the Gulf of Mexico become too chilly for the endangered Florida manatees, and these slow-moving aquatic animals head to King's Bay and the Crystal River area. This turquoise water paradise is accessible to humans almost exclusively by boat, and is protected specifically for these huge animals. The area's many natural springs create warm, shallow, crystal-clear pools and lagoons. Humans visiting the refuge are invited to kayak and snorkel with the manatees, but warned never to get too close or touch them.

Key

1 Tricolored heron
2 Manatee
3 Redfish

48

FLORIDA MANATEE

When they are not traveling through the water, manatees spend most of their time eating. They are herbivores, and graze on plants that grow underwater, such as seagrass. Manatees must swim up to the water's surface to breathe, which they do every three to five minutes.

Manatees are about 10 feet long and weigh between 800 and 1,200 pounds.

Manatees have very thick skin and three or four fingernail-like toenails on their flippers.

Manatees use their lips to grasp and pull seagrass and floating plants into their mouths, like elephants using their trunks.

The Florida manatee is a subspecies of the West Indian manatee, and a close relative of elephants.

Key

1. Northern parula
2. Florida panther
3. Black bear
4. American alligator
5. Pig frog
6. White-tailed deer
7. Wood stork

FLORIDA PANTHER REFUGE

This refuge sits in the heart of Florida's Big Cypress Basin, a vast swamp that stretches across south Florida. Visitors can hike established trails through grassy wetlands and hardwood "hammocks," or over slightly higher elevations on dry land. The refuge is home to the endangered Florida panther, which tends to hide in the shadows. However, other animals live here too. In the early morning or late afternoon, you might glimpse deer, bears, American alligators, and birds such as the red-shouldered hawk and the swallow-tailed kite. If you're lucky, you might come across panther tracks in the mud!

Discover this!

Towering cypress trees once dominated this landscape, reaching impressive heights of up to 130 feet tall, but they disappeared as a result of logging during and after World War II. The cypress swamps have slowly recovered as a new generation of trees has grown.

Watch this!

Red-cockaded woodpeckers are the only woodpeckers in North America that nest in pine trees. These southern birds peck and scratch for up to three years to complete a nest excavation in a living tree. They mainly eat other inhabitants of the same tree: the local insects.

Find this!

Tawny Florida panthers prey on deer, raccoons, armadillos, and rabbits. Dense brush makes an ideal place for secluded panther dens.

Find this!

Visit this swampy place in the heat of early summer and you might witness the ghost orchid in full bloom. These leafless, vine-like plants can often be found draped in the high branches of cypress trees.

The beautiful striped zebra longwing butterfly is the state butterfly of Florida. These slow-flying creatures live for several months—much longer than the average butterfly. They are known for their intelligence and memory.

Spot this!

Saw palmetto is a small palm tree that is native to this area. Its berries feed bears and deer, and are thought to have medicinal qualities for humans.

Watch this!

The acrobatic swallow-tailed kite catches flying insects by making sharp dives, rotating its tail. These birds also eat tree frogs, lizards, nestling birds, and snakes. Groups of kites, also known as "broods," "kettles," or "strings," gather at night to roost on branches.

MISSISSIPPI SANDHILL CRANE REFUGE

Wet pine savannas are flat, open grasslands with few trees. These wet forests are the only place in the world where the spectacular, seven-foot-tall Mississippi sandhill crane can be found. In 1975, one area was designated as a refuge, to protect this crane and its increasingly rare habitat.

Key

Discover this!

Longleaf pine trees have adapted to the naturally occurring fires that help this pine ecosystem regenerate every few years. Very young trees appear like fountains of dark pine needles—a fire can sweep over them without causing any harm. Mature trees grow layers of fire-resistant bark, which protects the tree during a blaze. Seeds are shed only after their pine cones have been warmed by a fire.

Don't touch this!

Several species of carnivorous plants live in the pine savanna, including the yellow pitcher plant. To get the nutrition it needs, this plant baits insects with nectar, then traps them with slippery leaves. Pointy hairs inside the leaf "cup" prevent an insect from escaping, and digestive juices at the bottom of the cup complete the job.

Spot this!

Toothache grass has corkscrew-shaped seed heads that bounce on the breeze. They flower only after having been exposed to fire. Some say if you chew on this grass, it has a numbing effect on the mouth, which is what gives the plant its name.

Watch this!

Sandhill cranes mate for life. Pairs share parenting duties—they incubate and protect their precious eggs together. Feathery chicks, also called "colts," hatch in the spring. They are ready to walk soon after hatching, and learn to fly at around two months old.

SALT PLAINS

Great Salt Plains State Park in Oklahoma is a beautiful, barren landscape. It formed from salt, left behind by a prehistoric ocean. The large, shallow, salty lake is stocked with catfish, saugeye, sand bass, and hybrid striped bass. The area is home to wildlife, but there is little vegetation. Animals in the park include white-tailed deer, eastern fox squirrels, American badgers, and porcupines. Large flocks of birds visit the area, feeding on fish and the salt brine flies that live around the water.

Key
1 American white pelican
2 American bison
3 American avocet
4 Black-necked stilt
5 Snowy plover

DID YOU KNOW?

Oklahoma's salty plains are the only place in the world where people can dig for ancient hourglass-shaped crystals of selenite. Some people believe that these crystals have healing properties.

Large flocks of American white pelicans move to Great Salt Plains Lake to feed during spring and fall. This is a stopover on their annual trip from the Great Plains to Mexico. As many as 70,000 birds show up at once for easy fishing in the shallow water. They stay for about two weeks before continuing their journey.

Discover this!

Watch this!

Salt brine flies are well adapted to this salty environment. They hatch in the water and serve as a source of hydration and food for the snowy plover and other birds in the area. These insects produce telltale bubbles when they dive into the water. When plovers see the bubbles, they wait, knowing a meal will soon appear.

Great Plains toads fill the salt plains with a piercing, chugging call on spring and summer evenings. It sounds like a loud, fast "chee-ga, chee-ga, chee-ga," that can last for almost a minute.

Hear this!

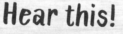

Spot this!

Bull snakes in this area often sun themselves along the trails and ponds on warm days. These bulky snakes are nonvenomous constrictors, and can grow to be eight feet long. They sometimes slither up trees in pursuit of rodents.

Muskrats are semiaquatic rodents that are native to the United States. These super swimmers can paddle backward and forward, and stay under water for about 15 minutes. If they need to rest, muskrats' dense fur helps them float.

The Oklahoma salt flats are an important nesting site for birds, such as the snowy plover. To make a nest, it scrapes out a spot in the sandy soil and lines it with bits of shell, grass, pieces of invertebrate exoskeletons, and pebbles. These nests are often disturbed by humans.

Be careful!

Find this!

Graceful, arching prairie cordgrass decorates the salt plains. It can grow up to eight feet tall and turns a beautiful bright-gold color in fall. Cordgrass seeds feed many animals, and its stalks provide shelter throughout the year.

DID YOU KNOW?

More than a million gray bats make Fern Cave their home each winter.

FERN CAVE

Fern Cave is a wild, dark place with over 15 miles of rocky, underground corridors, 18 levels, and a mysterious pit that's more than 400 feet deep. This spectacular and spooky place is an important winter home for a massive colony of endangered gray bats. The place gets its name from the rare and beautiful American hart's-tongue fern, which is also found here.

Key

1. Cave turkey
2. Eastern gray squirrel
3. Eastern cottontail
4. Gray bat

Wow!

Fern cave has a lot of water in it. At times, parts of the cave can only be reached by scuba divers. The cave is home to fish and other water-living animals, such as cave crayfish and the endangered Alabama cave shrimp, which is eyeless and translucent.

Find this!

Huge and evergreen, hart's-tongue fern grows through cracks in moss-covered rocks in the forested area around this famous cave. Its glossy fronds poke up through the snow in the winter.

Spot this!

Gray bats are furry, winged mammals that are at risk of becoming extinct. They look something like little furry dogs with wings. Gray bats hibernate in deep caves, such as Fern Cave, during the winter. In the summer they prefer caves closer to lakes and rivers. Bats use a process called echolocation to detect the flying insects they eat, such as mosquitoes. The bat sends out sound waves, then listens to see if any bounce back.

The Midwestern United States is famous for its wide, open prairies, where native grasses and colorful wildflowers sway in the wind. These vital grasslands are home to many important animal species, such as the iconic black-tailed prairie dogs. Prairie dogs peek out of their dens and use yips and barks to communicate with other members of their close-knit family groups, known as "coteries." The prairie is also home to badgers, bull snakes, and butterflies, such as the spotted regal fritillary. The Midwest region also stretches northward to vast, remote, and wild places such as the Boundary Waters Canoe Area Wilderness, in Minnesota. Here wolves, moose, bear, deer, and bobcats live in beautiful boreal (cold-climate) forest. Midwestern cities can be home to many animals, including deer, coyotes, and Canada geese.

MIDWEST

GREAT LAKES
BASIN

TALLGRASS
PRAIRIE

BEAR BLUFF BOG

DESOTO

TALLGRASS PRAIRIE

Wide-open, fertile grasslands are one of the planet's most important ecosystems. This habitat is home to rare birds, butterflies, insects, reptiles, and other small wildlife. Prairies are also important for the health of our planet. Roots from grasses store carbon, which helps fight climate change. Prairies are one of the most endangered habitats because it's easy for humans to build or develop agriculture on this flat, relatively dry land with few trees. The Northern Tallgrass Prairie National Wildlife Refuge was established to help bring the prairie back to Minnesota and parts of northern Iowa, and provide a place for wildlife. Summertime visitors will find yellow sunflowers and stalks of purple thistle waving in the wind. They might even hear the bark of a prairie dog standing guard on its mound.

Key

1 Black-capped chickadee
2 Prairie dog
3 Swift fox
4 Common wood-nymph
5 Prairie skink
6 Ground squirrel
7 Dakota skipper
8 Striped skunk
9 American kestrel

DID YOU KNOW?

Some people refer to the prairie as a "sea of grass." Prairie lands once covered a third of the United States, from Michigan to Montana.

Spot this!

The bobolink is a small songbird that flutters over the prairie, seeking shelter in the grasses and shrubs. Males sing a cheerful, bubbling song that starts with a buzz and ends with a high-pitched gurgle.

If you're out on the prairie and spot a dirt mound with a hole on top, it might be the entrance to a prairie dog burrow. The mound is a lookout point, to help these rodents watch out for predators such as coyotes or weasels. Mounds also keep rainwater out of the burrows. These underground systems branch out into cozy chambers and form "towns."

Wow!

Look at this!

Big bluestem grass grows more than 6 feet high during the prairie summer. It becomes a protective (and edible) host for small animals, birds, and insects such as the common wood-nymph— a butterfly also called the "google eye" due to its eyeball-like spots. Big bluestem turns gold and pink in the fall.

Snap this!

Male greater prairie chickens stage astonishing antics when it's time to find a mate. They journey to specific areas called "leks" or "booming grounds." Then they puff up orange sacs on their necks, drum their feet, hoot, jump, and cackle to impress the females.

Spot this!

The Dakota skipper is a small brown butterfly that lives among the prairie grasses, feeding on nectar from its favorite wildflower: the purple coneflower. This butterfly has disappeared from most of its habitat, and is in danger of becoming extinct.

Hear this!

The dickcissel is a common prairie bird whose warbling song sounds like "dick-dick-see-see-see." It perches on shrubs and hops around looking for seeds to pluck.

Prairie skinks are shiny lizards whose long tails fall off if they're caught by a predator. But don't worry—the lizard will grow its tail back over the next few weeks. Summer is the best time to see a prairie skink in action. The hotter the temperature, the faster the skinks can run.

Discover this!

DeSoto is a large, lush wildlife refuge that gives migratory birds a place to lay over during their long annual journey to their Arctic nesting grounds. Each November, as many as half a million spectacular white snow geese stop to rest and feed in the reclaimed wildlands along the Missouri River in Iowa and Nebraska. Bald eagles often arrive in the area after the snow geese. They stay for the winter and can be seen perching in the cottonwood trees.

Hear this!

Snow geese flock to this national refuge every November, and so do bird-watchers. The big attraction? Listening to throngs of birds honk, yelp, quack, and cry as they swirl in the air, land in splashy formation, and then take off again after eating.

Key

1. Snow goose
2. Canada goose
3. Bald eagle
4. American wigeon
5. Blue heron

Spot this!

Wood ducklings must jump into the water from their nests when their mother calls. Sometimes this means a leap of more than 50 feet. In summer, look for broods of colorful wood ducks learning to swim in DeSoto's wetlands and ponds.

Towering cottonwood trees get their name from the fluffy white stuff that protects their seeds. As the seeds disperse in the wind, these shady trees appear to snow.

Watch this!

GREAT LAKES BASIN

The Great Lakes Basin rests between Canada and eight US states. Ancient glaciers carved deep trenches that formed the five Great Lakes, which now hold most of North America's supply of fresh water. Conservationists and many others work hard to keep non-native species from disrupting this pristine and important ecosystem. The lakes are varied in nature and home to many types of wildlife, including huge sturgeon and other fish species such as the muskellunge and the northern pike. The forests, wetlands, and meadows around the lakes are home to many mammals and birds.

DID YOU KNOW?

Isle Royale National Park is a remote island wilderness in the middle of Lake Superior. It is home to gray wolves and moose, which the wolves rely on for food.

Key
1. Great blue heron
2. Moose
3. Lake sturgeon
4. Walleye
5. Wood duck
6. Beaver
7. Coyote
8. Gray wolf

Spot this!

Lake sturgeon are endemic to the Great Lakes Basin. That means this is the only place on Earth where they exist. An adult sturgeon can reach 7 feet long and weigh almost 250 pounds. They eat crayfish, clams, and leeches.

Boreal woodland caribou, found in the Great Lakes area, are a furry cousin of reindeer and other species of caribou that roam the Arctic tundra. Thousands of them once lived in these dense woods and rocky islands. Today, there may be as few as 30 of these animals left in the Great Lakes Basin region. They live in small groups, stay in the forest, and eat lichens, grasses, and shrub leaves.

Wow!

Watch this!

The Great Lakes Basin region is home to shiny aquatic salamanders called mudpuppies. These unusual amphibians breathe with their lungs, but also have feathery-looking gills that take in oxygen. They sometimes make a barking sound.

Playful river otters make dens at the water's edge and come out to fish at night. Their nostrils clamp shut underwater, enabling them to dive and swim underwater for up to 8 minutes!

Discover this!

Spot this!

You'll need a microscope to see phytoplankton, which are free-floating microscopic algae. These tiny plants live at the surface of the water. They serve as food for zooplankton (microscopic animals) and small fish. In turn, the small fish serve as food for crustaceans and larger fish that then feed even larger fish, birds, and mammals.

Watch out!

The walleye is a favorite of people fishing in the Great Lakes Basin. But watch out—it sports a mouthful of sharp teeth. This metallic beauty hunts smaller fish species, such as yellow perch and minnows. It eats local invertebrates such as crayfish, frogs, and mudpuppies.

Beavers change the environment to suit their needs. They build protected ponds by gnawing down trees. When a tree falls, they add mud and branches to block water. Once a pond forms, they build lodges out of mud, branches, and rocks, with underwater entrances.

Look inside!

American bullfrogs are named for the sounds they make—their deep croaks sound like a bull bellowing. They are the largest frog species in North America and can jump a distance of 10 times their body length.

Hear this!

DID YOU KNOW?

This area is home to many bird species including the American bittern, eastern wood-pewee, sedge wren, pine warbler, rose-breasted grosbeak, clay-colored sparrow, and Lincoln's sparrow.

Key

1 Black bear
2 American bittern
3 Sedge wren
4 Wilson's snipe
5 Fisher
6 Purple finch

BEAR BLUFF BOG

The northernmost part of Wisconsin points like a finger into Lake Superior toward Canada. It's a wet and wild habitat, and home to lots of important wildlife. Bogs like the one known as Bear Bluff Bog are often found in this state, especially at the edges of its many lakes—it's part of the Great Swamp of Central Wisconsin. Less waterlogged parts of the area are home to trees such as the yellow birch, black ash, and tamarack. Shrubs, moss, and ferns line the forest floor. Many species of birds live here, as well as black bears, fishers, and wolves. On a visit to this place, you will need to pull on some boots and enjoy the mud.

Smell this!

Skunk or swamp cabbage blooms even when there's snow on the ground. When its leaves are crushed, this plant gives off a rancid odor that reminds people of skunk spray or rotting meat.

MY NOTES

Hear this!

This vast and remote area is home to gray wolves. Each pack has a unique sound, and on a clear night their howls can be heard from 10 miles away. In this boggy habitat they often eat deer and beavers.

Spot this!

The sharp-shinned hawk is an agile forest bird, named for its ridged, featherless lower legs. This yellow-eyed raptor lurks in the shadows, ambushing its prey—unsuspecting songbirds.

Spot this!

Yellow-bellied flycatchers breed in this area's shady, swampy forests. These big-eyed birds make nests in low bushes and dart out to grab insects in midair. Both parents feed the babies.

In the shadows of this marshy area you'll find a soft, carpet-like green plant called sphagnum moss. There are many species of sphagnum, but they all seem to look very similar! This moss has been around since prehistoric times and can survive even if frozen.

Discover this!

Tawny cotton grass is part of a group of grasslike plants called "sedge" that grow in swampy areas. This kind of cotton grass is covered in puffy, white seed pods.

Beware this!

Black bears in this area gorge on berries and roots in summer. If you see a black bear, make sure to watch it from a distance. Black bears also eat insects, deer, and fish.

Touch this!

The Northeast is the area of the United States that is most populated by people. However, there is still room for a diverse population of native animals and plants. In Maine, harbor seals bask in the state's Atlantic Ocean harbors. Lobster boats have plentiful hauls, and shallow, coastal tide pools teem with barnacles, blue mussels, and sea stars, which hide in the slippery seaweed. At the New Jersey shore, beachgoers might spot humpback whales or bottlenose dolphins in the distance. In the beach dunes, ospreys nest on man-made platforms. Shore birds such as the red knot make an important stop in New Jersey, to refuel on horseshoe crab eggs as they make their way north on their annual migration route.

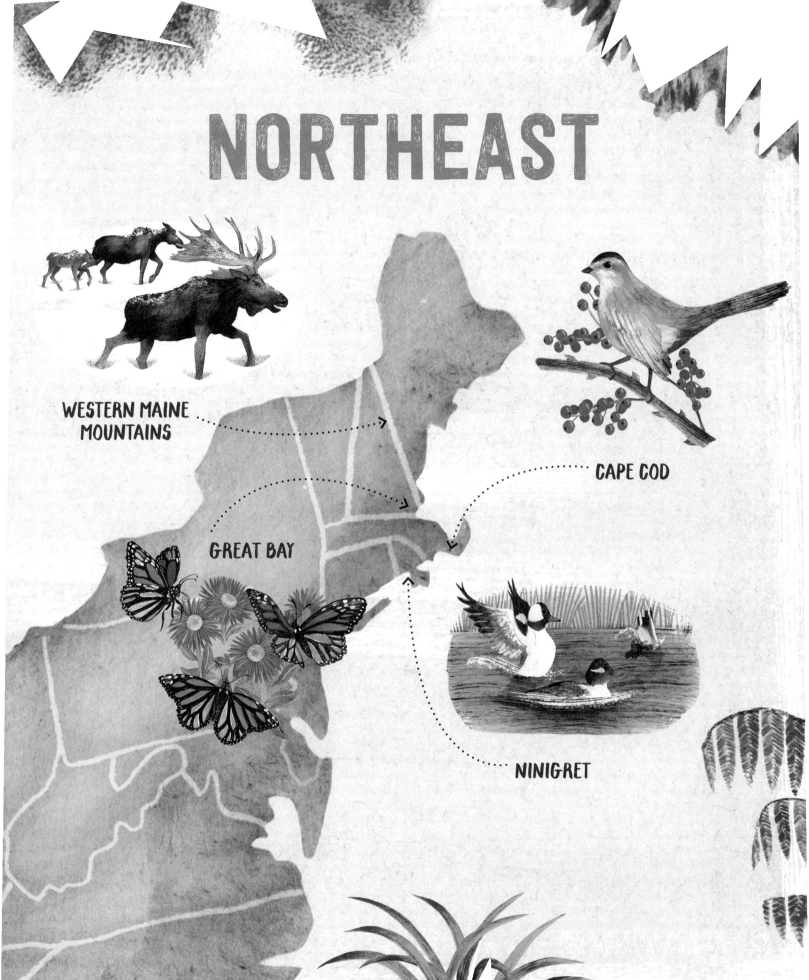

NORTHEAST

WESTERN MAINE
MOUNTAINS

GREAT BAY

CAPE COD

NINIGRET

WESTERN MAINE MOUNTAINS

The Western Maine Mountains straddle the border between New Hampshire and Maine. This is a region of extremes: tall mountains, bright wildflowers, and colorful fall foliage. Come winter, the area becomes cold and snowy. The nearby Umbagog National Wildlife Refuge is a vast forest area, home to hundreds of bird species, such as the gray jay, the boreal chickadee, and the spruce grouse, which is about the size of a chicken. This lake-filled area is also home to lots of fish as well as otters, muskrats, and beavers.

Key

1 Bald eagle
2 Moose
3 Boreal chickadee
4 Muskrat
5 Common loon
6 Great blue heron
7 Gray jay

Moose hooves are like snowshoes. They spread out to support the animals' weight in snow and mud.

Bloodsucking ticks carry diseases that hurt moose populations. Climate change has made the ticks more abundant.

MOOSE

These colossal creatures stand up to 6 feet tall, and have antlers that stretch from 4 to 5 feet across. Moose fill up on leaves and twigs from trees, including mountain aspen, mountain ash, and red maple. They can also wade into water to eat aquatic plants.

Find this!

Visitors to this northern area can get up close and personal with native bird life by walking or paddling a kayak or canoe. Look for soaring bald eagles, wading great blue herons, and songbirds such as yellow-throated vireos.

Look!

American martens are pointy-eared relatives of skunks, otters, and badgers. They spend the winter in dens: snow-covered shelters under fallen trees. In summer, martens hang out high up in trees, sleeping on open branches or in abandoned squirrels' nests.

Spot this!

Summer coat

Winter coat

Snowshoe hares sport brown fur with black-tipped ears in the summer. In the winter they turn white, to blend in with the snowy landscape. Hares hide in dense brush to avoid predators such as American martens, foxes, and coyotes. Snowshoe hares have bigger bodies and longer ears than rabbits—they are a separate species.

Hear this!

The common loon communicates in wails and hoots. Loons thrive on Maine lake life: there is fresh water and plenty of fish. These birds are agile swimmers; they can catch and swallow fish underwater. A pair of hungry loons and their chicks can eat about 250 pounds of fish in a month.

GREAT BAY

New Hampshire's Great Bay is a 6,000-acre tidal estuary—a partly enclosed body of water that contains a mixture of saltwater from the ocean and fresh water from rivers and streams. The Great Bay Wildlife Refuge sits on the bay's eastern banks. Its geography is a puzzle of coves, woodlands, and wetland habitats. These protected areas provide a home for plenty of wildlife, including birds of prey, porcupines, and grasshoppers. The waters of the bay are home to underwater jungles of aquatic eelgrass.

Key

1. Bald eagle
2. Ring-billed gull
3. Wild turkey
4. Black duck
5. White-tailed deer

Track this!

Porcupines spend most of their time in trees, coming down only after dark. They are the second-largest rodent native to the United States (after the beaver) and are covered with hard, sharp protective quills. A baby porcupine is called a porcupette. Its little quills harden about an hour after birth.

Beautiful orange-and-black monarch butterflies eat the nectar from bright-purple New England asters. In turn, these butterflies serve as a food source for mice and birds, while spiders and ants prey on monarch butterfly eggs.

Spot these!

Many bald eagles spend winter in this snowy area because it has fish and waterfowl to eat, little human disturbance, and plenty of trees for roosting in.

Meet this!

Families of wild turkeys can be heard strutting down wooded paths—and even sometimes the roads—in this area. The adults gobble, yelp, cluck, and cackle to communicate.

Hear this!

Spot this!

Wildlife video cameras in this refuge catch unexpected antics, such as southern flying squirrels gliding from tree to tree after dark. When the sun goes down, this nocturnal species busily collects acorns and hickory nuts. The muscly parachute-like skin that allows them to glide is called the patagium.

Find this!

Park rangers in this wildlife refuge encourage American kestrels to move in by setting up nesting boxes. The kestrel is the most common falcon in North America and also the smallest. It eats grasshoppers, lizards, and small birds.

Discover this!

Shimmery green eelgrass offers an underwater sanctuary for marine residents including delicate young oysters, crabs, and scallops. It also provides a safe place for fish such as Atlantic cod to lay their eggs. The eelgrass also buffers the shore from the impact of waves, which helps to prevent erosion.

Hear this!

Visit this refuge on a spring evening and you'll hear noisy spring peepers celebrating the arrival of warmer weather. These little tan, brown, and gray frogs are easier to hear than to see—they are about the size of a quarter.

NINIGRET

Key

1 Osprey
2 Eastern bluebird
3 Striped bass
4 Gray fox

Watch this!

Bufflehead ducks dive underwater to snap up insects, snails, and water plants. These small, colorful ducks beat their wings quickly in flight, and rock from side to side.

The Ninigret National Wildlife Refuge takes its name from a Narragansett Indian chief. The area sits on the shoreline of a huge salt pond area. It contains many kettle ponds that were carved out by glaciers, millions of years ago. This watery refuge is a great place for bird-watching. Ospreys fly over Ninigret Pond looking for fish to eat. Bluebirds perch in native shrubs and feed on insects and wild berries. Ferns grow in the cool shade of white pine and oak trees. In the summer, you'll find humans using the clear waters of Little Nini Pond for swimming.

Spot these!

American woodcocks have gone viral on social media with videos of their mating dance, which involves buzzing, whistling, and kissing noises. These shorebirds have cinnamon-colored feathers on their underparts. They can be found at the edges of forested areas and wetlands.

Hear this!

The common yellowthroat is one of the most abundant nesting birds in Ninigret's shrubs. Listen for males, who sing a distinct rolling song that sounds like "wichety-wichety-wichety."

Discover this!

Broad-leaved cattail is native to this area's wet soils and shallow marshes. Some Native Americans have used its roots and shoots for medicine. Its fluffy insides were used to stuff mattresses.

CAPE COD

Cape Cod National Seashore's vast and beautiful beaches are a popular destination for family vacations in the summer. This area is home to more than 450 species of animals including amphibians and small mammals. Birds seem to run the place. Egrets hunt for fish in the salt marshes, and hawks pluck prey from the dunes. Stocky piping plovers dash this way and that in the surf, pecking for food such as insects, worms, and mollusks that live under the sand's surface.

2

3

...NOW?

...ape Cod is a ...ook-shaped peninsula off the Massachusetts coast. It was named after the big-headed Atlantic cod, a fish that was once abundant here.

Key

1 Snowy egret
2 Common tern
3 Piping plover
4 Atlantic white-sided dolphin

Smell this!

Beach heather is a shrub that is found among the dunes at the Cape Cod National Seashore. It carpets the ground and helps prevent erosion. Fine hairlike structures on the scaly leaves protect the plant from the wind and sun.

Find this!

The Eastern spadefoot toad is one of 12 amphibians found in these sandy surroundings. Speckled and covered with tiny warts, it spends most of its time buried underground. To help burrow into the earth, it has small spade-like bumps called tubercles on its back feet.

Hear this!

Gray catbirds hop from branch to branch while making loud meowing calls. Sometimes they sing from inside the protection of a thorny hedge. Their gray color is accented by a dark-gray "hat" and deep-red bottom feathers.

Taste this!

Cranberries grow wild in this area's wetlands. The plants have pink blossoms in the spring, which then become berries and are eaten by birds, deer, and rodents. Humans have cultivated the sour berries in bogs for generations.

Spot this!

White-footed mice are the most common mammal at the Cape Cod National Seashore. These mice often live inside fallen trees and are excellent swimmers. They eat seeds, acorns, and insects.

You might have more wild neighbors than you realize. All sorts of animals share our backyards, including predators such as foxes and bobcats. Some birds might live in your yard year round, while others may pass through on their way to somewhere else. Which animals share your backyard depends on where in the country you live.

Desert backyard

Birds such as western screech owls often nest in the cavities of saguaro cacti. Bobcats are most active in the desert around dawn and dusk, and enjoy napping under backyard shrubs.

Woodland backyard

Chipmunks often burrow in grassy areas, in backyard woodpiles, and under sheds. The hawks, foxes, and snakes that might also live in your neighborhood prey on these small striped rodents.

Suburban backyard

City and suburban backyards are home to wild animals too. White-tailed deer might congregate in grassy areas, while cottontail rabbits take cover under bushes. By day, flowers attract wildlife such as honeybees and bright-yellow goldfinches, who love to peck at dried seeds. Coyotes, foxes, and opossums walk down empty streets at night.

Tropical backyard

In tropical locations such as Florida, you might share your backyard with many beautiful birds, such as blue herons and pale-pink spoonbills. Starlings and egrets make nests in backyard palm trees. Frogs, snakes, lizards, and butterflies are common. If you live in the south, your lawn might even be visited by a wandering American alligator.

INDEX